Richard Scarry's
First Little Learners

Cars
and Trucks

DIFFERENT PEOPLE, DIFFERENT CARS

Mr. Paint Pig
needs a truck with
lots of space to
carry paint and
brushes.

mouse in
a racing car

The Cat family likes to
drive in an open
four-seat convertible.

mouse in a pencil car

Sergeant Murphy drives
a bright red motorcycle.

Bananas Gorilla likes
his yellow
bananamobile.

Creamer Cat delivers fresh
milk in his yellow van.

three bugs in
a green leaf car

flying pickles

dashing vintage roadster

Postman Pig picks up mail
in his mail van.

mailbox

great big tractor-trailer pickle truck

The Pig family
drives in a
station wagon.

Lowly Worm always
drives his apple car.

Harry Hyena
on roller skates

9

AT THE GARAGE

Greasy George's garage is a busy place for cars to be repaired, washed, and filled-up with gasoline.

Greasy George

A car having a bath.

happy mechanic

Gasoline is delivered to Greasy George's garage
in this tank truck.

delivery man

underground gas
tank

gas pump

Mother Cat's car gets a full tank
of gasoline, and a clean windshield.

CARS AND TRUCKS FOR BUSY HELPERS

siren radio

The policeman needs a speedy car to get quickly where he is needed.

white ambulance
to carry patients
to the hospital

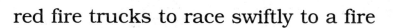

red fire trucks to race swiftly to a fire

tow trucks for repairmen...

... and for
repair women

jingling bells

There is an ice-cream truck!

IN THE STREET

Here is a TV truck.

Here comes the garbage truck,
picking up
garbage.

garbage can

There goes the
street sweeper,
cleaning the street.

Here is an Army car.

There goes a scooter...

... and there is
Mr. Frumble in
his pickle car.

Mind your
hat,
Mr. Frumble!

BUSY MACHINES

Here is a bucket scoop, digging a ditch.

the surveyor's plan

a marker string

Earmuffs protect against the noise.

A compressor compresses air for the jack-hammer.

a detour sign

The jack-hammer digs up the pavement.

cone

Here is a crane,
laying a pipe.

crane
operator

driver

Here are two
busy workers.

Hey! Stop
chatting!

a jeep

steam-shovel
dumping rocks

tractor
dumping earth

bugdozer

an all-terrain
buggy

dump cart
carrying earth

18

dump truck
not watching
where it dumps

bulldozer
pushing earth

Here is the school bus,
carrying children to school.

WHICH CAR WOULD YOU LIKE TO DRIVE?

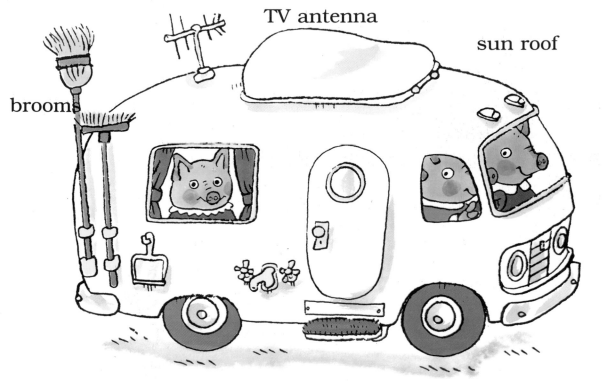

TV antenna

sun roof

brooms

The Pigs' camping car?

Mr. Fixit's hammer car?

mustard

Wilbur Rabbit's
hot dog car?

20

Tommy's taxi?

Captain Salty's boat car?

A bug car?

Sprout Goat's tractor?

Or Dingo Dog's sports car?

Drive carefully!